The Moon Was Blue

A collection of illustrated poems for all the family

By

Penny Turner

The content of this book, including all illustrations and poetry by Penny Turner, Penny Poetry & Art are covered by copyright. No part or whole of this work or any other work created by Penny Turner should be duplicated in any way without the agreement of Penny Turner

Published by P Turner

This book is dedicated to:

My wonderful parents who have given me everything – including the key to the door of imagination.

My dear husband without whom nothing in my life seems possible, and my brother who always believes in me.

I thank and love you all. x

Introduction

I am often asked where I get the ideas for my poems and pictures. I can only answer truthfully and from the heart and say "from my imagination." I have always had the ability to go to a place where imagination lives... a place where mats can fly, where fun characters get up to mischief, and all in a parallel world to ours. It's a doorway through which I can go at any time of the day or night and it's somewhere you can go too. You may be standing at a bus stop, sitting perhaps in your bed, or maybe eating your tea, but whatever the time or the place, the door to imagination is always there – all you have to do is look for it, reach out to the big brass door handle, then step forward.

INDEX
1. I'd Like To Post An Elephant
2. Lilly And Her Bubble Gum
3. Don't Wake The Woo
4. Doris And Dodger
5. George The Giraffe
6. My Pet Dinosaur
7. Four Little Mice
8. Rose
9. The Magic Mat
10. Mrs Wren
11. Archie And His Tail
12. Teddy bears One, Two, Three
13. My Special Umbrella
14. Ted
15. The Magnificent Ride-On Stegosaur
16. The Little Teapot
17. Little Bird Blue
18. Who Put That Polar Bear There?
19. Lucy And Her Rocket
20. Lester And His Roar
21. The Lion, The Tiger And Leopard
22. Are Clouds Really Sheep?
23. Robbie's Christmas Wish
24. Pirates
25. The Mouse And The Monkey
26. Time For Bed
27. Teamwork
28. The Moon Was Blue
29. Floss The Naughty Fairy
30. The Cloud
31. The Crusty Lemon Curd
32. Barry
33. My Star

I'd like to post an elephant: first class I think is best

Don't Wake The Woo!

Don't wake the Woo
Whatever you may do
'Cos the Woo will get grumpy
And poke his tongue at you!

Woos are quite mean
And oh so very keen
To cause lots of mischief
Wherever they have been.

Don't wake the Woo,
The tales I've heard are true,
Their manners are a big disgrace
And they're shocking through and through.

So don't wake the Woo
'Cos you haven't got a clue,
There's nothing worse
He'll hiss and curse
So please don't wake the Woo!

Doris And Dodger

Doris and Dodger were sitting on guard
Bathed in the moonlight in Finnegan's yard.
Starting their shift on a crisp winter's eve
Dogs on patrol as their masters take leave.

"Doris," said Dodger, "I feel that tonight
We may have the pants of a burglar to bite!"
"Well Dodger," said Doris, "you're not often wrong,
I could do with some fun so I hope it's not long..."

The minutes ticked by as the dogs did their rounds
Checking the yard and listening for sounds...
Then excitement came over the wily old pair
And Doris she winked as a scent hit the air.

Burglar! She grinned and answering the call
The pair made their way to the perimeter wall,
And descending a rope and quite unaware
Was a felon about to discover the pair!

"You get his leg, Doris, I'll get his rump,"
Said Dodger the moment his teeth neatly sunk,
And Doris she grappled with sweaty old sock
But this lady made sure that her jaws had a lock.

The burglar shot up, in obvious pain,
And dogs hanging on the material strained.
With the ripping of trouser and sock in his ears,
The burglar succumbed to his dread and his fear.

He scrabbled and scrambled and bit on his lip,
But try as he might his foothold just slipped,
As Doris and Dodger hung in delight,
To his leg and his rump in the winter moonlight.

A yell and an OOOOOHH, and another loud tear
And the burglar shot up and flew through the air.
Like an acrobat star he shot to the sky
And landed streetside as a policeman passed by!

Doris and Dodger had triumphed once more,
Adding success to their tally and score.
Burglars nil, top marks dogs on guard,
Doing their duty in Finnegan's yard.

George the giraffe was in need of a scarf,
As he found it quite chilly up high

George The Giraffe

George the giraffe was in need of a scarf,
As he found it quite chilly up high,
Being so tall was no fun at all
With his neck and his head in the sky.

The problem you see – of course, naturally,
Was to find one to fit him just right.
Most were too small and would not fit at all
And would prove to be itchy and tight.

So we went to the shop to see what they'd got
And asked the assistant's advice.
George squeezed in the door,
Then on the shop floor,
We admired what they had and the price.

The assistant was kind but we still couldn't find
A scarf that would fit a giraffe.
The colours were bright, the designs were just right
But the fit of them looked rather daft.

Then the tailor next door said that he was quite sure,
He could help with a stitch here and there,
And scarfs in a row, he started to sew
And he asked George to sit on a chair.

George was amused as a ladder was used
So the tailor could stylise the fit.
Then all there agreed he looked handsome indeed
In his customised colourful knit.

Back at the zoo, friends all wanted one too
When they saw George so terribly smart.
So now at the shop they do mail order stock
Of extra-long scarfs for Giraffes!

I have a pet dinosaur under my bed,
Don't ask how he fits there with such a big head.

My Pet Dinosaur

I have a pet dinosaur under my bed,
Don't ask how he fits there with such a big head.
He only comes out when I'm all on my own,
And he's terribly shy when my family's at home.

Ferocious and nasty is what I have read,
But that's simply not true it has to be said,
As Dennis my dinosaur's a real friendly chap,
Not aggressive at all – a real pussycat!

Dennis got lost one day on a walk,
He took a wrong turn when the road took a fork,
And somehow he managed to cross over time,
But he doesn't know how, as there wasn't a sign…

But Dennis is happy under my bed,
With the fluff, and the books, and my grumpy old ted.
And I think he will stay, and not worry I'm sure,
That today he's the last of the great dinosaurs.

Fidget, Poppet, Rolo, and Boo
Woke up one morning with nothing to do.

Four Little Mice

Fidget, Poppet, Rolo, and Boo
Woke up one morning with nothing to do.
They ran round the house and played hide and seek,
But Mother was cross with them under her feet.

"Out you must go children, play where you will,
You're so very noisy and never sit still!!
I've got washing and darning and dinner to cook,
And dusting to clean every cranny and nook!"

Squealing and laughing they tumbled outside.
They ran through the field that was long and so wide.
Down to the Farm House so far away,
The four little mice had been travelling all day.

Darkness was suddenly starting to fall
And a worried expression came over them all.
Out of the darkness a menacing yowl
Alerted them all to a cat on the prowl.

"My goodness!" said Fidget, and Boo gave a scream,
"That cat sounds so hungry and terribly mean.
Why did we travel so far from our home?
We're totally lost and all on our own!"

Just then a voice familiar and kind,
Was heard in the distance somewhere behind.
They hugged one another. "Its Mother!" they cried,
Then took to their heels and ran for their lives.

All out of breath and fearful they met,
Their Mother was full of remorse and regret.
"Never again will I tire of your play,
Your noise and your laughter that rings out each day.
Nothing is dearer than you precious four,
I'm so pleased to know you are all safe once more."

Rose has found her toes,
And counts them every day.

Rose

Rose has found her toes,
And counts them every day.
Just in case by any chance
One may have run away.

The thing with toes,
As everyone knows
They wiggle all the time,
And it's hard when you are counting them
To keep them in a line.

And what she will do
When she takes off a shoe
Is to count them all once more.
In case one is hiding just inside
She's only making sure!

At night when toes are out of sight
Beneath the cotton sheet,
Rose will count them in the dark
Before she goes to sleep…

A dog, a rabbit, a mouse and a cat,
Went for a ride on a magic mat.

The Magic Mat

A dog, a rabbit, a mouse and a cat,
Went for a ride on a magic mat.
Off to a land that was very flat,
And everyone there wore an oversized hat!

Of course they all decided to get
Their own four hats – a matching set,
Of colourful brims for the dry and the wet,
That they lifted to greet whomever they met.

And now they live in the land that's flat,
The dog, the rabbit, the mouse and the cat,
All are happy and that is that,
In their oversized hats with their magic mat.

Mrs Wren had children ten,
That she added to just now and then.

Mrs Wren

Mrs Wren had children ten,
That she added to just now and then.
Her house was lined with feathers soft,
From the kitchen door to the small wee loft.

Mrs Wren was a mother hen
And would fuss her children numbered ten.
And hug them daily bye and bye,
As back to the house they all would fly.

Archie was a mouse with a very long tail
And others would step on it, making him wail

Archie And His Tail

Archie was a mouse with a very long tail
And others would step on it, making him wail,
Of course not on purpose, but then all the same,
A tail of such length was a terrible pain.

He tied a red ribbon all neat in a bow
On the end of his tail so others would know
To step over his tail and keep it in mind,
But still they would catch it quite often, he'd find.

Then in a drawer one day just by chance,
A long curly corkscrew he happened to glance,
And winding his tail around it at night,
He hoped it might help with his terrible plight.

By morning his tail was the talk of the town,
As now it was shorter and all curled around,
The shape of a corkscrew all twirly and neat
And well out the way of everyone's feet!

Teddy bears one, two, three,
Will come on a picnic with me.

Teddy Bears One, Two, Three

Teddy bears one, two, three,
Will come on a picnic with me.
Our knapsack is packed, our sandwiches wrapped,
So it's off to the woods for our tea.

We have found a nice spot in the shade,
So I pour out the sweet lemonade.
We sit in a row,
Bears like this you know,
With a clean table cloth neatly laid.

My bears all have manners so fine,
The best you will see when they dine.
Sitting up straight in front of each plate,
My bears one, two, three, in a line.

I own a special umbrella, and just where the handle is hooked,
I stand and hold onto it firmly, then gently I insert my foot.

My Special Umbrella

I own a special umbrella, and just where the handle is hooked,
I stand and hold onto it firmly, then gently I insert my foot.
As the silvery raindrops start falling, like pearls from out of the sky,
My umbrella lifts slowly and upward, together we both start to fly.

Off to a land full of wonder, where waterfalls shimmer and shine,
Where raindrops have smiles on their faces, and splashing in puddles is fine.
A place where despite all the water, no one will ever get wet,
And rainclouds are ever so friendly, and some people keep them as pets.

Me and my special umbrella, we stay out for most of the day
Coming back home in the evening, where neatly I fold it away.
It hangs in the hallway in waiting, ready for forecasts of rain.
When me and my special umbrella will be off on adventures again.

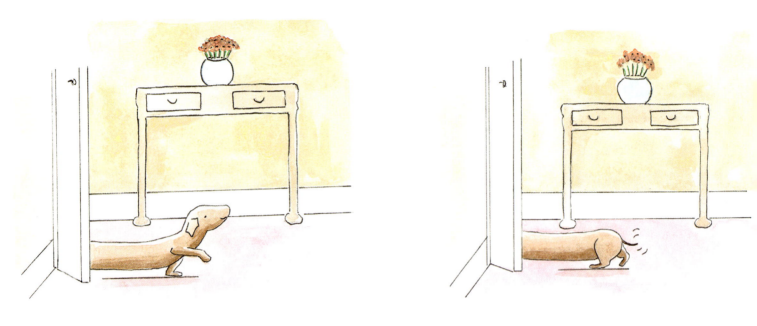

Ted left the room ten minutes ago,
But because he's so long it seems terribly slow

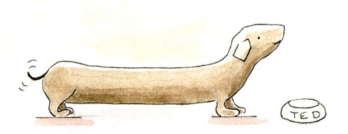

Ted

Ted left the room ten minutes ago,
But because he's so long it seems terribly slow
For his tail to catch up with his head in the hall,
And sometimes they don't ever meet up at all!

Ted is quite used to not seeing his tail,
It's a life where a few little drawbacks prevail.
A sausage dog's lot can be testing it's true,
But with a body so long what's a poor dog to do?

However, dear Ted is quite used to his lot,
And just doesn't care if he's in or he's not.
When his head's in the sun, his tail's in the shade
And when you think that Ted's left, you find that he stayed!

Every caveman's dream machine,
This mode of transport had to be seen!

The Magnificent Ride-On Stegosaur

Every caveman's dream machine,
This mode of transport had to be seen!
Full of style from head to floor,
The magnificent ride-on stegosaur.

Air-conditioned, you could feel the breeze,
You could seat a family with total ease.
Parking was very easy too,
Being so high you got an all-round view!

Taking on fuel at any stop,
And shopping, well you could pack the lot!
Holidays and trips abroad,
All made possible with a stegosaur!

They'd pop to Saurbones Stego lot,
For part exchange or Dino swap.
Pick their model and when they were sure,
Just drive away their Stegosaur!

Out in the garden overgrown,
Sat a little teapot all alone.

The Little Teapot

Out in the garden overgrown,
Sat a little teapot all alone.
Slightly cracked and very sad,
He dreamed about the life he'd had.

Used each day in pride of place,
With cups so fine and cloths of lace,
He sat upon the table proud,
His spout to pour that steamy cloud.

But old and damaged here he sat,
Wishing he could turn time back.
To be of use in such a way
To brighten up each lonely day.

And then a bird so wee and small,
Came along that day to call.
"I need a house," she said, "for me,
And all my lovely family."

A home for those who'd love him still,
And soon with precious things they'd fill.
And the teapot came to smile once more,
And no longer cared for his life before.

Don't you cry, little bird, please don't be sad.
I'm sure that your story is not so very bad

Little Bird Blue

Don't you cry, little bird, please don't be sad.
I'm sure that your story is not so very bad.
Your feathers look fine and your wings good and strong,
I'm sure, little bird, that there's nothing much wrong.

Don't sob, little bird, look the sky is so blue
And all of your friends are waiting for you.
All will be fine when your tears fade away,
The sun will come out on this beautiful day.

Dry your face, little bird, and spread out your wings,
Clear your throat and let's hear you starting to sing.
You are not on your own and we all care for you,
All is really quite well my little bird blue…

It was an odd kind of morning that morning,
The kind when your socks just don't match.

Who Put That Polar Bear There?

It was an odd kind of morning that morning,
The kind when your socks just don't match.
The household was cramming the bathroom
And the toast was determined to catch.

The dishwasher rumbled and rumbled,
The dog barked away at the door,
And rubbing my eyes, from my sleep over night,
I couldn't be sure what I saw.

Well, needing the jam from the larder
And still not awake it was true...
I opened the door, and looked in once more,
And that's when I thought I'd ask you.

"Who put that Polar Bear there?" I said.
And the rest of the family said, "WHAT!"
"In the larder," I said, "as big as you like,
Eating the cake that he's got!"

Well, all of them doubted my question,
And thinking I'd just made it up,
They decided that they would open the door,
So they queued up to all take a look.

"Who put that Polar Bear there?" they said.
And I was relieved I can say.
Mornings were never the best in our house,
And this was the strangest of days...

What's to be done? We all sat and thought.
A decision would have to be made.
After all, it would mean a big weekly shop,
And a much bigger bill if he stayed!

Cont...

But mornings are busy, and time it was short,
So we all thought we'd ask of the bear,
If he thought that our larder was his sort of home,
And would he be happiest there?

Well he was so thrilled, and more than obliged
That he said he would help with the chores.
And to cover his stay in our larder,
He would clean out some jars with his paws.

Thank goodness! A crisis averted.
The larder was something we'd share.
But we never did sort out the mystery,
Of who put that Polar Bear there?

Lucy And Her Rocket

Lucy built a rocket
From cans and bottle tops
She built it in the garden
In a great big cardboard box.

Her family asked her plainly,
"Where do you plan to go?
Will you call us when you land
And kindly let us know!"

Lucy donned her goggles,
Her mittens and her coat,
And looking very focussed,
These words she calmly spoke...

"I'm going to the Milky Way,
My trip is planned and set.
I've got my chocolate sandwiches
And a hat, should it turn wet!

I don't suppose the journey
Will take more than a day,
After all it can't be hard
To find the Milky Way."

Lucy climbed aboard her craft
And gave a wave or two,
Then her rocket headed for the stars
And quickly out of view...

Well neighbours said,
"She's just a child, will she find the Milky Way?
And do you think she's likely
To make it home today?"

Cont...

Lucy built a rocket
From cans and bottle tops

But all the many doubters
They had to be contrite,
When Lucy and her rocket
That eve came into sight.

Burning through the atmosphere,
Her sturdy rocket flew.
Landing in a whirl of smoke,
She soon came into view.

Well neighbours clapped
As mom and dad were proud and overcome,
And Lucy had prepared a speech to read to everyone;

"I've seen the Milky Way," she said,
"I've seen the moon and stars,
But I think the nicest planet still,
Is definitely ours…"

A lion is king, a lion is proud,
With a mighty roar that is very loud

Lester And His Roar

A lion is king, a lion is proud,
With a mighty roar that is very loud,
But Lester is less than his normal self,
With a roar that's a squeak like a tiny mouse!

He had a roar but he's lost it now,
He's really not sure just when or how?
It sounds rather careless for a lion to lose,
And it's not a predicament he would choose…

Well, he asked in the jungle, he asked on the plains,
But the answer came back exactly the same.
No one had found a roar anywhere,
And no one would take it – they just wouldn't dare!

Feeling quite low and feeling quite glum,
He asked for the local physician to come,
Who declared in a moment, why your throat it is sore,
That's why you've lost your very loud roar!

What a relief, what a success
And something that nobody else would have guessed.
A spoonful of tonic and not a drop more
And Lester has found his mighty ROAR!!!

On a lovely day in the jungle
With nothing that much an ado

The Lion, The Tiger And Leopard

On a lovely day in the jungle
With nothing that much an ado,
The lion, the tiger and leopard
Met up in a clearing they knew.

Well, it was rare they all got together,
With time just to laze and to chat,
And they got to the subject of each other's coats,
And they decided to swap, just like that!

"I've always admired your wonderful mane"
Said the tiger, now looking so grand.
Wearing the coat of a lion,
The king of animal lands.

"I just love all these stripes..." said the leopard,
Admiring himself head to toe,
Parading around in the tiger's rich clothes
Like a star from top fashion show.

"These spots are so wonderfully different,"
Said the lion with heavenly glee.
"No longer so plain and one colour,
No one would recognise me!"

By evening they all bade a fondest farewell
And reluctantly changed back once more,
And the lion, the tiger and leopard
Looked exactly the same as before.

"Why can't sheep fly?" I asked.
    "Well," you said

Are Clouds Really Sheep?

"Why can't sheep fly?" I asked.
"Well," you said,
Whilst scratching your head,
They aren't really built for the task...

"But they look like they could," was my reply,
And you explained the reason why a sheep can't fly
At the gate of the field where we stood.

"They don't have wings!"
It was true and I was confused,
And you now laughed and looked somewhat amused,
At the logic applied to such things.

"And clouds don't have feet!"
You tried once more
As we reached the threshold of our front door.
So thinking quite hard, I took a seat.

And the minutes passed on my doorstep seat,
Watching the clouds in the summer sky
For any that might have feet...
And then I deduced it was purely a case
Of the wrong type of day for flying sheep!

Robbie was gripping a letter
Addressed to 'Santa – North Pole'

Robbie's Christmas Wish

Robbie was gripping a letter
Addressed to 'Santa – North Pole',
And in it he asked for one present,
That he wished for with all of his soul.

He hoped that this wish may be granted,
And putting it into the post,
He thought of the words he had written
And the present he wished for the most.

'Dear Santa, what I'd like for Christmas,
I hope you can sort out for me,
I just want a home and an owner,
Just someone to love me, you see.

I hope that you won't be too busy,
I hope that it's not hard to do,
But a home would be lovely for Christmas,
Which is why I am writing to you...'

"Pirates!!!" yelled the captain
Going shaky at the knees

Pirates!

"Pirates!!!" yelled the captain
Going shaky at the knees
At the sight of Jim the pirate king
The terror of the seas.

One eyed Jim and all his gang
Were standing on the deck
A motley crew of brigands
With a mind to run a wreck.

"Give us your treasure!" said Jim with a grin
Showing his teeth that were black and quite grim!
"Shiver me timbers, there's booty aboard
And me and the boys will be taking the hoard!"

The captain said meekly, "Now you listen here."
His knees still knocked loudly as he trembled with fear.
"You really should go before we get quite rude,
We can be so aggressive when we're in the mood!"

But Jim wasn't worried
He'd tackled the best
He had already spied the big treasure chest.
His flag, skull and crossbones, was raised with a yank
And he said, "Yo me hearties, who's for walking the plank!"

The Mouse And The Monkey

The mouse and the monkey
Flew away on the end of a bright balloon,
They packed some clothes and a basket of food
With a knife, a fork and a spoon.

Over the trees they sailed away
Over the roof tops red.
"What a clear day," remarked monkey to mouse.
"Clearer than clear," he said.

They flew to the clouds so way up high
By the birds and the bumble bees,
They left all the ground so way behind
And the rivers and racing seas.

On they travelled holding so tight
To the string of the bright balloon
And floated through rainbows caught in the light
And the morning became afternoon.

Way past the sun so warm and bright,
Way past the moon by a mile,
Till on a star they came to rest and picnicked for a while.

"What a day we've had," said the mouse so proud
And filled his cup to the brim,
"What a day away for friends like us," he said with a beaming grin.

And then as the night began to fall
They took hold of the bright balloon once more
And drifted gently homeward bound
Through the starlit sky without a sound.

Time for bed little sleepy head
 Time to dream away

Time For Bed

Time for bed little sleepy head
Time to dream away,
All tired out from hours of fun
Of make believe and play.

Time for bed little sleepy head
Let's tuck you in so warm,
Your little eyes are heavy now
As you begin to yawn.

Time for bed little sleepy head,
Now we tiptoe from your side.
Drift till morning on a gentle wave
That's sailing a dreamy tide.

Off went their owners in the car,
And minds they turned to the well-stocked jar

Teamwork

Off went their owners in the car,
And minds they turned to the well-stocked jar
Of dog treats that sat on the kitchen side...
But some thinking would need to be applied.

Dogs, though, are clever, and dogs they are keen,
And the treat jar was truly their ultimate dream.
So some teamwork they thought may do the trick,
To spill out the contents and take their pick!

It wouldn't be naughty, it wouldn't be bad,
Their owners would surely be glad that they'd had
The forethought to have some lunch through the day
In the brief interlude that they were away...

The Moon Was Blue

The moon was blue, all soft and pale
As I hitched a ride on a giant snail.
We sailed a lake, its waters pink,
With a friendly cat in a kitchen sink.
We sailed, and sailed, and sailed away
Till the night became the colour of day,
And met a bird with rainbow wings
That flew us home on lemon strings.

Here comes Floss the naughty fairy,
Her wand is bent and her hair is scary.

Floss The Naughty Fairy

Here comes Floss the naughty fairy,
Her wand is bent and her hair is scary.
Floss gets up when it's time for tea,
This is not at all how a fairy should be!

Floss casts spells and they all go wrong,
And talks in class for far too long.
She'll forget her homework, just you see,
This is not at all how a fairy should be.

Floss plays tag with the dragonflies,
She hides in the clouds so way up high.
She teases the wasps in the old tall tree.
This is not at all how a fairy should be.

Her dress is torn and never neat,
She won't wear shoes upon her feet.
Mischief makes her full of glee,
OH FLOSS! This is not at all how a fairy should be...

Don't rain on me cloud, it's rather unfair
That you'd rain over here, but it's dry over there...

The Cloud

Don't rain on me cloud, it's rather unfair
That you'd rain over here, but it's dry over there...
The sky is quite blue just a wee glance away
But over my head you've turned horribly grey.

Now let me just say that today is not good,
As I didn't assume that you possibly could
Be as mean as can be, when I'm dressed for the sun,
Getting moody and raining when I thought there'd be none!

If you come back tomorrow – well I'll better prepare,
I'll put out some boots and a rain hat to wear.
We could talk through what's made you feel so sad and grey,
But please little cloud, don't start raining today...

"Land ahoy!" said the bird.
"That's not land," said his friend

The Crusty Lemon Curd

"Land ahoy!" said the bird.
"That's not land," said his friend,
"Haven't you heard?
That's the Crusty Lemon Curd!"

"The Crusty Lemon Curd," said the bird,
"What on earth and sea,
And how absurd,
A floating Lemon Curd..."

"Where is it from, this massive pie?"
Said the bird to his friend.
"Why, from the sky
It fell one day," he did reply.

"And now 'tis home to the wild Blue Honk,
And even the Purple Goat
Has made his home
On the pie that floats."

"Well," said the bird in true dismay,
"What wonders we do find at sea.
There's very few this day have heard
About the Crusty Lemon Curd..."

My invisible hippo called Barry
Is a friend like no other I know.

Barry

My invisible hippo called Barry
Is a friend like no other I know.
I found him one day in the wardrobe,
Now he follows wherever I go!

It's hard to insist to my family
That the settee is now out of bounds,
That Barry is watching the TV
And likes to stretch out in the lounge.

In school he sits quiet in assembly
But at lunch it's so hard to explain,
Why the apples and squidgy rice pudding
Will constantly run out again.

His appetite's ever so healthy
And when shopping it's so very hard,
He's squeezed in the trolley Mom's pushing
So I have to be quite on my guard!

He'd eat up the whole veg department
In the big supermarket in town,
So I have to be doubly careful
And remind Mom that Barry's around!

At night he sleeps back in the wardrobe.
Quite a relief I can say...
As my bed is really not suited
To a hippo that's snoring away...

At night when I should really be all tucked up in my bed,
I look between my curtains at the dark sky overhead